TABLE OF CONTENTS

FOUR

This book comes about as unprecedented human movement

leads, here as elsewhere, to conflicts, suspicions, and opportunities

to reconsider what is meant by "the foreign," by "the foreigner."

It is also a very personal account of negotiations across borders

(between languages and cultures, between one species and all

the rest, between health and sickness, between poetic forms, and

between self and others).

Core Samples from the World

OTHER BOOKS

BY FORREST GANDER

NOVEL

As a Friend

POETRY

Eye Against Eye

The Blue Rock Collection

Torn Awake

Science & Steepleflower

Deeds of Utmost Kindness

Lynchburg

Rush to the Lake

TRANSLATIONS

Spectacle & Pigsty, by Kiwao Nomura (with Kyoko Yoshida)

Watchword, by Pura López Colomé

Firefly Under the Tongue: Selected Poems of Coral Bracho

Connecting Lines: New Poetry from Mexico

The Night: A Poem by Jaime Saenz (with Kent Johnson)

Immanent Visitor: Selected Poems of Jaime Saenz (with Kent Johnson)

No Shelter: Selected Poems of Pura López Colomé

Mouth to Mouth: Poems by Twelve Contemporary Mexican Women

ESSAY

A Faithful Existence: Reading, Memory & Transcendence

Core Samples from the World

FORREST GANDER

With Photographs by

Raymond Meeks

Graciela Iturbide

and Lucas Foglia

A NEW DIRECTIONS BOOK

Manufactured in the United States of America
First published as a New Directions Paperbook (NDP1199) in 2011
Published simultaneously in Canada by Penguin Books Canada Limited
New Directions Books are printed on acid-free paper.

Design by Malcolm Grear Designers, Providence, RI

Library of Congress Cataloging-in-Publication Data

Gander, Forrest, 1956-
Core samples from the world / Forrest Gander ; with photographs
by Raymond Meeks, Graciela Iturbide and Lucas Foglia.
p. cm.
ISBN 978-0-8112-1887-0 (paperback : acid-free paper)
I. Title.
PS3557.A47C67 2011
811'.54 — DC22

2011001154

10 9 8 7 6 5 4 3 2 1

New Directions Books are published for James Laughlin
by New Directions Publishing Corporation
80 Eighth Avenue, New York, NY 10011

Core Samples from the World

"No one is stranger than the self. Which appears as another and comes to haunt us by accepting, finally, one of many invitations."

— Enrique Lihn (Forrest Gander translation)

"There is the hidden presence of others in us, even those we have known briefly. We contain them for the rest of our lives, at every border we cross."

— Michael Ondaatje

"The surprising finding of Watts and Strogatz is that even a few extra links are sufficient to drastically decrease the separation between the nodes. These few links will not significantly change the clustering coefficient. Yet thanks to the long bridges they form, often connecting nodes on the opposite side of the circle, the separation between all nodes spectacularly collapses."

— Albert László Barabás

"The astonishing night, the foreigner among humans."

— Friedrich Hölderlin (David Constantine translation)

ONE

for Valerie Mejer

It's not an insult to refuse to drain the glass, she tells me
And a fly crawls from the bowl of salsa picante.

Would you choose to bury the organs with the child?
And he retreats to his room and closes the door.

Here, birds in the zócalo whiz and tweet like children's toys
And there, a charred corpse hanging from the bridge.

From the seat behind her, the boy pokes his sister's head with a plastic fork
And getting no response, tests it on his own head.

Would you kindly turn the damn wipers off, the attendant asks
And the odor of manure and wet hay hits us.

A kind of mystery adheres to those who have suffered deeply
And thank you Mr. and Mrs. Radiance.

It sounded like the chimmuck of a rock dropped into a stream
And the piston-driven breathing of sex.

The couple at the bus station—when had we kissed like that?
And *Nice evening—Yes it is—A bit skunky—That's for sure.*

Terrorist and victim circle the last chair as the music stops
And the worm's valved mouth snapping.

When I rise out of myself into occasion, I said
And when do you rise out of yourself into occasion, she asked.

Late enough to count moths at the window
And the boy will be coming up the porch steps when he comes.

The long row of treadmills choiring
And above them, televisions replay the disaster.

Where are you going? Ghosted with dust. From where have you come?

Dull assertiveness of the rock heap, a barren monarchy.

Wolfspider, size of a hand, encrusted with dirt at the rubble's edge.

What crosses here goes fanged or spiked and draws its color from the ground.

Xanthic shadow at the edges.

Where are we going? Ghosted with dust. From where have we come?

Stretcher loaded with clods by a spavined work shed.

What does it mean, a cauterized topography?

One step forward and he is with us. One step back, another realm absorbs him.

The sense of epoch loosened, unstrung.

Each one thinking it is the other who recedes like a horizon.

The miraculous cage visible under his skin.

I cannot be discarded, his eyes say.

A flute that plays one note. A face.

In the open pit at noon, men waning in brightness.

I can be read, say the rocks, but not by you.

The air burnished, almost mineral, like a thin peel of mica.

Mound in the photograph, iris in the eye.

What does it mean, a cauterized topography?

To salvage rocks the color of all else from all else the color of rock.

I can be read, say her eyes, but not by you.

As if the land had abandoned itself.

Rain-flushed from denuded hills, the soil powders in wind.

One step forward and we are with them. One step back, another realm absorbs us.

Don't pick up the rocks, he says, because rocks belong to the dead.

Xanthic shadow at the edges.

The distance flat as horsehair plaster, all depth sponged away.

Black knoll of tailings.

There is nothing between his eyes and ours, not even invitation.

Each stone carrying its death sentence into the animate world.

Fly maggot eating the red ant's brain.

The sense of epoch loosened, unstrung.

Light broken off in the air.

The twig's shadow has the same quality as the shadow of a man.

Glance held, an afterglow.

All depth sponged away, the distance flat as horsehair plaster.

Iris in an eye, mound in the photograph.

Don't pick him up, rocks say, because the dead belong to the rocks.

Encrusted with dirt at the rubble's edge: wolfspider the size of a hand.

A man's shadow has the same quality as the shadow of a twig.

What crosses here goes fanged or spiked and draws its color from the ground.

The air burnished, almost mineral.

XINJIANG

THE PAMIRS POETRY JOURNEY

Twenty poets speaking seven languages on a field trip to the outskirts of Beijing. A birdless summer day, no insect whirr. Entering the gate of the Summer Palace as a pack and dissolving into pairs. Without his Chinese-Persian translator, Emran Salahi is pensive, tight-lipped. He leads the way through the Hall of Dispelling Clouds, past its discolored statuary and fusty tapestries symbolizing eternal power. Then, dawdling in the corner of a side room, peers around a painted screen and discovers a white-haired man face-down on a table strewn with syringes.

Behind everything

the foreigner sees, something he doesn't

know how to look for.

Yukio Mishima telephoned Kazuko Shiraishi a week before his death, flirting, she divulges as we walk along the Summer Palace lake. Like Allen Ginsberg, whom Shiraishi also knew, Mishima spent his final days calling friends. Although it's muggy enough to sweat, smog diffuses direct sun and no one slings a shadow. Not now, not any time in Beijing. Shiraishi pauses beside a gnarled juniper to stare at what appears to be a casino boat on the lake. Columned, canopied, its interiors painted with delicate floral patterns, the whole thing carved from ocherous marble. Yang Lian ambles over, telling the story: *Instead of buying the armaments her militia requested, the Empress Dowager drained the treasury and built them a beautiful stone boat.* Now Emran Salahi joins the group, nodding toward the useless boat docked forever at the shore. He tries out his minimal English.

That thing, he

says, it is

like a poem.

As Chinese poets, we don't want to go backward, Xi Chuan observes, but ahead of us the way forks in innumerable directions. Forgetting which language he has just heard, but remembering the substance, the exhausted translator begins to translate the original language into the original language. The nonnatives are inept at reading the forms of discussion here, much less the subtleties. What is taken as evident wafts away. Tensions come clear, faces shaking *no*, one translator interrupting another. The topic, *Where is Chinese poetry going in the age of globalization,* invites phatic responses. But under their masks of muteness, the visitors go beyond listening to; they listen *into.*

What else is being

asked, what

is at stake?

After the Beijing conference, half the Chinese poets head home to jobs and families. The rest fly with a posse of foreigners to Kashgar in western China's Xinjiang Autonomous Region. Stepping down to the tarmac, each is aliened, each is opening. The plane from which they disembark, the only vehicle with wheels on the runway. According to plan, a young guide introducing himself as Abdul leads a trip to the shrine of The Fragrant Concubine, a Uyghur beauty whose legendary natural body odor, intensified by camel milk baths, made her a favorite of the Quianlong Emperor. Because in local versions of the legend she resists the emperor, longing to return to Kashgar, she is revered by Uyghurs ill-at-ease with Han Chinese rule. Abdul announces the next stop, the famous Kashgar Market where *everything but milk of chicken* is sold. A labyrinth of stalls that display ancient Chinese and Roman coins, Pashmina wraps and scarves, dry toads wide as umbrellas, bins of walnuts and ripe cherries, cheap Pakistani suits, traditional Uyghur hats made in Italy, bolts of striped silk, jars of saffron, pelts common and exotic, and fragrant peaches. There are hanging carcasses harassed by flies at butcher stands one beside another and, at every corner, pomegranate vendors beside marvelous juice-presses ornamented in silver and wood.

Men at the edge of

their shops, spitting on fingertips

to seal the deal.

In Kashgar, prior to a meeting with regional writers, the poets pay respect to the great eleventh-century Uyghur scribe Yusuf Has Hajip whose 12,290 line poem, "The Wisdom of Happiness and Pleasure," helped codify a Uyghur ethos. His tomb, Abdul explains, was destroyed during the Cultural Revolution, rubbled. Who did it? Han soldiers? No, Abdul says, glancing at his feet; his own father, a Uyghur shoemaker, helped to batter down the tomb.

Their minds,

he says,

were altered then.

Near Hajip's tomb, workers who have been demolishing a fifteenth century *siheyuan,* a compound of wooden houses, plop down in the debris to remove shoes and wash feet and hands. Although there's a mosque nearby, there hasn't been a call to prayer. The Chinese government permits mosques, but not *ezan,* the public prayer-song. When the faithful empty out, the prayer room reclaims silence: unadorned walls, a thin red carpet, the odor of feet. Since thousands of non-religious Han Chinese have been moved to Kashgar as part of a "develop the west" campaign that has rebooted the local economy and desertified the purlieu, major political and cultural changes—as well as stopless winds—are perturbing Xinjiang Province.

In the fifties, five severe sandstorms, in the sixties,

eight, in the seventies thirteen, fourteen

in the eighties, in the nineties, twenty.

The famous Kashgar animal market takes place only on Wednesday. Discrete tracts for goats and sheep, for horses, and for cattle. Thronged with pedestrians and carts, men on horses, women shouldering enormous loads. Freshly slivered watermelons quickly sepia with dust. A butcher draws his blade across the plush throat of a goat lying on its side, its legs bound. His foot on the animal's face keeps the head pointed upward, the throat defenseless. A surprise, how gently it dies, convulsing only a little, then again as he cuts deeper. The head quiet under the shoe,

> Blood spurting neatly into a hole
>
> in the concrete platform over which
>
> the meat stall has been hauled.

At a welcome breakfast with the Communist Party brass at the army mess hall, a large calligraphic poem (about horses and beauty) by Mao hangs from one wall. Afterwards, a bus rushes the writers to the town of Artux to share in the celebration of its twentieth anniversary. In a large plaza before a new and apparently empty convention center, all the town's children, grade school through high school, are seated on portable stools in groups demarcated by the color of their caps. Military men and officials on either side of the raised stage are flanked by hot air balloons that sway from their moorings. Adults fill out the rear, standing as far back as the road, maybe four thousand altogether. Asked to read something to the crowd, Emran Salahi recites a poem in Persian, but prefaces it with a sentence in Turkish that the Uyghur audience, stupified to find they understand him, clamorously applaud. Then in Uyghur and Mandarin, official speeches stretch into early afternoon. The sun stalks around the convention center and hits everyone full-face. A wave of boredom slumps the crowd. Finally, after compulsory applause, cages are opened and pigeons released, veering maniacally as

> Fireworks burst above the crowd, scattering
>
> sparkle that flutters down
>
> into the fust of gunpowder.

After Artux comes Yingsar, a knife-factory town, and then Yarkand, an ancient city on the Silk Road where, in the 10th century, Queen Amannisa Khan compiled the defining anthology of Uyghur poetic songs known as the *Twelve Muqam.* From Yarkand, the bus grinds away from Uyghur territory toward the Kyrgyz Autonomous Prefecture and its culture of desert horsemen. Hustled into a small town hall, the foreigners are treated to an evening of song and dance from the *Manas,* a 232,162 line Kyrgyz poem (twice the length of the *Iliad* and *Odyssey*) memorializing the Kyrgyz fight for independence against the neighboring Uyghurs. Each of the local singers specializes in a single section of the poem, one declaiming in a raspy voice at a martial clip and another chanting forlornly, but all strumming the three-stringed komuz. The last *Manas* singer rocks back and forth, reciting his part in the meter of horse hooves, trochaic tetrameter. After the performance, the poets are invited to sit cross-legged at long tables in a restaurant where, in their honor, a horse has been slain and cooked. Baijiu, a liquor the unacculturated might mistake for industrial fluid aged in a goat bladder, is liberally served in miniature, frequently refilled glasses. After each toast, the glass must be drained and held mouth-out to the others to display its expenditure, that same gesture of proof requisite in porn movies. (Here, as everywhere, male bonding is acted out as a kind of coalitionary self-destruction.) Meanwhile the tables fill up with horse, skewers of yak, large fish, duck, chicken, fatty lamb in spicy sauce, and pigeon with noodles, to name only the meats. A goat head and a large knife are passed around from hand to hand. The host digs out and eats an eye before offering the head to the poet to his right. It's a kind of Kyrgyz machismo that dictates

> The head
>
> must be stripped
>
> to bonewhiteness.

GOBI

The driver arm-wrestles the gearshift through the Seven Colored Mountains, through the Gongur Mountains, and then the bus shudders and pings to a stop below the White Sand Mountains where travelers drink tea at a roadside stand selling medicinal herbs. Half a dozen adolescent girls are playing cards beside the highway, their eyebrows painted—in accordance with a tradition so continuous it's mentioned by eighth-century poet Li Bai—a fetching shade of green. Along roiling, concrete-colored rivers in the mountains, the bus diesels past government-built bunkers and Kyrgyz stone-and-hide houses. The road arrowing into the Gobi. Poplar woods thin into a belt of sand, red willow bush, thorn, and jiji grass. Individual camels appear, then small caravans of camels.

Here and there, a shepherd

stands cipherlike

in the barren expanse.

KOK BORU

The local Kyrgyz custom of Down Horse Drink, Up Horse Drink is translated into a series of compulsory toasts each time the poets board and exit the bus. Town officials have mustered in the middle of the road to welcome the writers who step down and are handed shot glasses of baijiu by young women in traditional dress. Musicians blow and strum. Down Horse Drink. The poets climb back into the bus. Shot glasses of baijiu are handed through the windows. Up Horse Drink. The bus rumbles to the center of town where the guests are queried: Who can ride a horse? Then they are whisked by van to the desert to witness the Kyrgyz version of a polo match, played with the decapitated carcass of a goat. Those who can ride are given mounts from which to survey the tumultuous competition, men grappling from the saddles of their galloping horses for a hold on the carcass. Behind the yipping riders, in the distance where a new mining facility squats in the Haoshi Bulak ore field and where the rocky plain, plowed and abandoned, lies denuded, a stupendous dirt cloud rises, mixing with dark purple sky. One competition framing another. The riders have not given up, but the storm is barreling theatrically toward them, their clothes snapping in wind like a fire.

And below the mounted spectators, the nervous

horses begin to champ and snort

and turn.

TWO

for Coral Bracho and Marcelo Uribe

In increments enunciated (Oh) within

      where the meanings (in increments) lie

bare (she says) (Oh, to her friend)

      who is watching (I am watching) a cat slink

(while we walk) keeping pace with us

      through the fenestrated walls (adobe) of

a ruined house (Oh, this finger) in the village

      where she grew up (her accent

makes clear) *This finger,* she says,

      delighted, holding it up,

has a heart in it! (Pulse)

      And thinking I don't see (the friend), she

takes (from her purse) a toothpaste tube

      (purse open) as she walks (we walk)

(where's the cat?) along the soft

      path between (adobe) walls,

squeezes toothpaste

      on her finger (with its heart) and smears

it (looking away) against her upper

      and (still looking away) lower teeth

then touches me (with her breath)

for C

Through my torso, the smooth

diffusion of aguas ardientes. Another

shot. Dawn.

Fan whir covers distant

rooster crow, dog bark cuts through fan whir.

That the world has you in its time? Is that what

she said? Meaning I too

drank from the glass on the night stand, swallowing

the spider before I knew

I'd seen it?

Two

girls in heels and

communion dresses

cross the window, their necks

bent shyly down.

Glancing at my watch, I turn back

to the *hechicera*, her face ashen, whirled

with lines. *You still haven't told me*

if she'll recover, I say.

You have the eyes of —, she

repeats twice, not finding the word. Then,

De donde viene?

*　　*　　*

So the present
hoses itself out. And with it —

Sitting in the lobby of the clinic,
its walls painted
like children's rooms with starfish

and trains and jungle birds
and the children shuttling back and forth, the nurse
calling their name and a few words

in English or Spanish, the children
taking their mother's
or father's hand,

trailing the nurse past
a registration desk, down
the hall, the sequence of closed doors,

toward the one door open. Radiance inside. Bald
children wearing hats, and a bald baby in a mother's arms, and
here in the lobby, where I wait for you

to be X-rayed,
some stranger whose exhaustion
can't be fathomed, begins to snore. If *this*

is the world and its time, as irrevocably it is,
when I step out into sunlit air
suffused with sausage smoke and bus exhaust,

with its relentless ads
for liquor and underwear,
where am I then?

Quien es? First words
of *Hamlet.* Last
of Billy the Kid.

Who is it on her knees in the Tepito market
screaming for money, naked to the waist,
operatic, arms raised to expose
double mastectomy scars?

Who is the *traga-años*, swallower
of years, selling me lottery tickets
in a tortilleria, a wrinkled
Mazatec in a red
t-shirt with the words *Fresh*
Fruit Delicious across her chest.

And who was it the surgeons narcotized
before excising a chunk of muscle and cancerous
flesh over my shoulder
blade and grafting the hollow
with a sheet of my own skin the breadth
of a paperback, assuring me later
the wound would fill in with blood and
flux so now,
twenty years later, this *salsa de chile de arbol*
makes my scar throb?

MALINALCO

Invited by one of the clinic regulars
to a wake for his child, I'm pressed
to the coffin in which the dead girl lies
dressed as an angelita. Her brothers
herd into the hall where *la señora anciana*
bestows each with the talismanic
name of an animal or bird. Late

                    in the evening,

at the bar of a restaurant known for its *sopa
de maiz con tabasco*, I find you eating
with your fingers. Your neck, when I
kiss it, smells like plantain
and oregano.

Who's there? you ask.

＊　　＊　　＊

To welcome the

strangeness of

strangers

not versions

simply of

my own

thought.

Through

the interpreter,

the Tzotzil shepherdess

indicates she has

some questions

too:

Tell me

how

is your lost

bird that was

found?

✶   ✶   ✶

Have you been to Africa?

Just the north.

Have you been to China?

Yes.

What took you there?

I was looking for bonds.

Have you been to France?

I have.

How do they live?

Like everywhere.

They have sheep?

Sure.

How many might one shepherd have?

I don't know, thousands.

How could they be counted?

You've got me.

What did you say?

I said I'm not sure.

And what took you there.

I was looking for bonds. I wanted to break a mirror. I wanted to render myself accessible, available. I wanted to borrow eyes from another language. I was looking for the words to come.

And now?

And now what?

And now that everything in your life has changed?

Synthesized with a common
helplessness. Fined-down
by the exorbitant demand of work,
surrounded, inundated with chatter
as the zócalo is
when grackles descend en masse
whirring, wheedling, scrawking. For us,
every hour has become that
hour of riotous distraction
swallowing us when we leave
for the clinic or my translation
job and swallowing us again
when we return in the evening to
Mexican sitcom laughter.

A boy walks the cobbled
street leading a rachitic blind man. *Lazarillo*,
he calls the boy. But the chatter
pulls in all directions at once.

And then you and I are standing at the bus stop
near Theater Hijo del Cuervo,
and a middle-aged woman is asking us
were we just there,
at the performance of *Krapp's Last Tape*.
She holds a hand to her throat. It made me,
she begins, and then she uses a word
I've only read, *aspirar*. Aspirate. Draw in.
And in the thin light we see she is crying.

Letting go your hand at the corner

and hurrying to piss in the cornfield,

I pass two men coming back

from pissing in the cornfield. *Going*

to sing a song? one of them calls to me.

The wound, they say, fills in. Blood and flux.

Wasp on the rock wall

measuring a translucent

quartz grain with its mandibles—

by which we know

below the funneled neck of the wasp's nest

a vermiform larva curls

against the paper wall, half-

paralyzed.

Tenga presente. Keep

in mind.

So many plastic bags snagged

in grass and cacti and bushes along the hill,

the landscape looks like an art installation.

That woman at the bus stop with her palm

to her throat:

the exigence of our dying

for access

to our own nakedness.

*   *   *

You have the eyes of —.
I was speaking to the bird on the low branch.
De donde viene?

Grace's warbler—he's little
but he pishes-in real well.

Had I just translated *Siento que mi fatiga se fatiga* as
My get up and go done got up and gone?
Something my mother used to say.
Then fell asleep for twenty minutes on a bench
in the zócalo and woke refreshed. As
though a door had been left open
from last night's bad sleep
and it was sufficient to return only
long enough to close it.

Came-to with a memory of lying
in your lap as you stroked my ears.
Bewilderingly sexual.

Grackle ruckus covers bootblack brush, organ
grinder cuts grackle ruckus.

*　　*　　*

But cannot

take my distance from it —

the sow asleep at the edge of

the clay lot, a pariah

dog bowing to suckle

the sow's swollen teats.

Sound of TV cartoons

carrying through the scrim of jungle

into the pyramid complex.

Through my mother, who was a weaver,

I thought I learned patience,

but as I approach slowly,

slowly, to identify the source,

thinking *I don't know, I'm not sure, we'll see,*

the metallic clicking in the piñons — insect? frog? bird? *Quien es?* —

changes pitch and

stops altogether.

Whether we are looking or not—

as in Julio Castellanos' painting,

"Angeles robachicos": the woman

sleeps by her husband with her hand

between her breasts while

two mestizo angels, weeping

silver tears, exit the house

through the window

with her swaddled infant.

— *Tenga presente.*

The world shifts

on a hairline crack. All last summer

you and I met for lunch in a clearing

we didn't know the locals call

The Girl's Grave.

✶　　✶　　✶

Revealed always

in situation. In Chiapas, the *hechicera* warned me,

they will approach from the left. *What?*

                                   Signs.

Returning again

to the ever-iterated assertion

of myself. And myself

with you. Weeks of slack,

then pop-up

moments of attunement.

Just beyond, the road clears

the jungle. Wind-

blown sands scarf the road.

We can't begin

to track the changes that

bring us here. Marriage

is only what continues

to be entered into. A door

opening, a face

peering around it. At El Chiflón

we park and get out to

train binoculars on

a beehive box

in the black mangroves.

Coasting into the swamp

from our left, a bare-throated

tiger-heron. Taking us

in, its huge yellow

iris blinks.

＊　　＊　　＊

— ever-iterated,

    the monumental claim to

the significance of —

                Come again,

        the waitress calls to a woman

    who, standing up from the table

           where she dined alone,

      answers, *We* will.

  Quick as a hummingbird.

Weaving sprigs of lavender, yarrow,

    mint and citronella into its nest.

           And the orchard

     laned with warm afternoon

              sun as two girls

    in communion dresses, returning

      from church, cross the window.

      Evening covers their shadows, your

        eyes cut the evening.

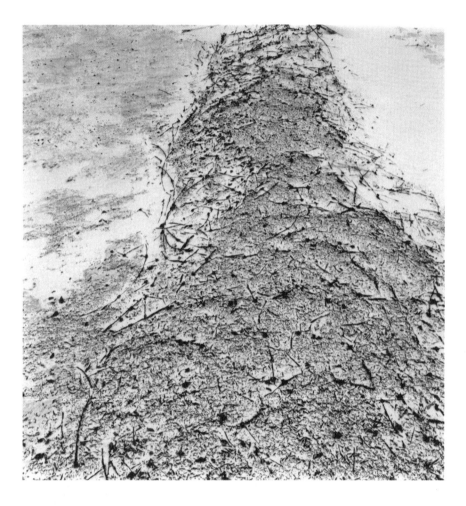

MEXICO

A CORE SAMPLE THROUGH 24 HOURS

Still here in the pre-boarding lobby of this tiny municipal airport in the Chihuahua Desert, waiting for a plane. Between the lobby and the tarmac where now, finally, *gracias a dios,* a plane is sitting, there are two alarmed doors. For the past four hours, the alarms have been loudly chirping to each other every ten seconds. Outside, adjacent to the tarmac with its one plane—

A big sycamore and boat-

tailed grackles

flying in and out of its branches.

The straggler is *exangüe,* utterly drained after two days of canceled flights, rerouted planes, and an all-nighter in the Houston airport. But two in the afternoon sees him joining his Mexican friends (and their friends) at a restaurant in San Luis Potosí.

At sixty something, Julieta, the woman sitting across the table, has indigo eyelids that shutter her eyes when she speaks and—whispers a local man—the most famous legs in Mexico, "legs as famous as Marilyn Monroe's." *¿Por qué?* Because in 2006, in one of the largest bull rings in the world, a half-ton bull named Pajarito, Little Bird, burst from the gate and leaped—in YouTube videos of the event, it looks like he's flying—over the heads of journalists, over the safety barrier, and up into the most expensive seats in the arena. On no other occasion in the sixty-year history of the arena had a bull jetéd out of the ring. In the unprecedented pandemonium that followed, Julieta was upended and gored, her legs exposed to everyone. The near-death experience made her an instant celebrity. *Corridos* were written and sung to commemorate her encounter with

Pajarito. Her shoe—which she lost ringside—was safeguarded in the arena office until, when she left the hospital for a party celebrating her recovery,

She was startled by two

officials tendering, on a silk pillow,

her forgotten shoe.

Saying, in conversation with actor and writer Aline Davidoff, *Pero allá puedes escribir cualquier que te quiera.* Speaking of the Banff Translation Center in Canada and meaning that *there, you can write whatever you want to write.* But by making a mistake with the subjunctive conjugation, saying instead: *there, you can write whatever loves you.* Aline looks up quizzically from her *cabuche,* the yellow fruit of a barrel-biznaga cactus.

In *her* presence, someone warns, *el ambiente se cargará electricidad,* the air will carry an electric charge. After lunch, offering the taxi driver directions, she stands so close to the window of the car that only her shapely torso is visible. It's raining and the spiked, aromatic scent from nearby creosote bushes is dizzying.

A cure for dizziness? the driver turns his head, incredulous. He says,

Para todo mal: mescal.
Para todo bien: también.

(For anything bad at all: drink mescal.
When better than before: drink more.)

Late afternoon, trailing some locals to the town of Santa Maria, famous for its rebozo weavers. In the zócalo, a barbaric, metallic *grackle*—the English name for the bird is onomatopoetic—saws into the steady, soft-shoeing of doves. A light breeze, through which the sun lances the nape of the neck, carries the scent of concrete dust, mangos, and dog shit. What else? Cheap radio songs, the complaining and claiming calls of children, church bells, swatches of adult voices, a gong from somewhere behind the church, and the sussuration of trees, their upper limbs twisted and white, juggling birds through their leaves. At the corner shop, stacked boxes of *piloncillos*—pyramidal molds of unrefined sugar—hum and flicker with yellow jackets.

On the other side of the zócalo, the tortilleria. Which is to say: two adolescent girls at either end of a machine that screeches—from 6:30 a.m. to 7 p.m. at night, when finally they click it off—like a train braking, braking, braking, and still coming on.

This rebozo, the weaver points out, smoothing it over her shoulders and chest, *is rapacejo.* Fenestrated? The incommunicable in another language: how to break that seal?

In early evening, the writers gather in San Luis Potosi for a round of readings. Veracruz poet Francisco Hernández, with his dog poems, is the crowd-pleaser. As the hall clears, the foreigner hurries up the stairs to the second floor, looking for a bathroom, and after a long futile search, returns to the balcony. The building is empty but for him and, below, one couple; the poet from Mexico City barks at her boyfriend, *Al paredón—Up against the wall!*

> An accompanying erotic gesture
>
> repossesses that phrase forever
>
> from police and executioners.

Que güeva, she mutters when she notices the gringo stumbling down the stairs. The phrase might be translated *What a drag,* but with its particular disappointment aimed at the testicles.

There's a congregation around the *puestos* across the street. One sign reads *DVD Semi-Original.* Two *puestos* away, the competition's sign reads, *DVD Clon.*

Así es la vida, tiene garra. Life's like that, the poet from Mexico city says as she and her boyfriend brush past, *it's got claws.*

One by one, the writers are haled from dinner tables to the front of the room where the mayor, putting down his microphone and picking it up again afterwards, shakes hands. An assistant presents each writer with a lapel pin of San Luis Potosí's coat of arms: a saint on a hill penetrated by three mine shafts. In fact, Mexican novelist Jorge Hernandez explains in a whisper, walking back to the table, the hill depicted on the pin is Cerro San Pedro, whose population has been protesting the reopening of open-cut mines and the use of cyanide in mining operations so close to their pueblo. If the Canadian company trying to reopen the mines succeeds, Jorge goes on, losing control of his volume, the iconic hill is going to be lopped away.

Across a plate of grilled nopales, Ysabel Fernandez Galán introduces herself as a museum director and asks who would like to see her museum after dinner—it's already past midnight and all but the dessert plates have been cleared. She has the key, she says. A warm, light brown face and soft grey hair. The impromptu invitation provides an excuse to escape the endless dinner party through which costumed characters, formerly posed as statues in the entry hall and on the stairs, have begun parading among the tables: the turbaned, white-robed facsimile of Indian poet Rabindranath Tagore, a gauzy Scheherazade, a nearly naked Maya Prince strapped into an enormous green-feathered headdress, a dietarian version of Gabriel Garcia Marquez (played by a local carpenter), Sor Juana Inez de la Cruz, and, among others, the famous nineteenth-century poet Manuel José Othon (whose nearby house has been turned into a rather antiseptic museum). The characters continue to vogue their way among the dinner guests in the enormous, high-ceilinged hall where the city's famous *quinceañeras* have been celebrated for a century. The band is striking up another standard nightclub number and a fifteen-man choral group in tuxedos tries once again to croon and gesticulate their way into the audience's tequila-tinged susceptibility to schmaltz.

Half an hour later, at the gate to the grounds of El Museo Francisco Cossio, Ysabel presses a button in a call box. A uniformed guard develops out of the darkness, greets her, and swings open the gate. Within,

A spit-groomed,

colorless garden lit

by a nearly full moon.

White totemic statues—they have the same prehistoric-postmodern appeal of sculptures in the Dongba God Garden in Lijiang, China—line the cobble walk-way. The museum was formerly a palatial private home. A second guard, inside, opens the front doors and all step into the foyer—two glass cases of fossils and rocks flanking the door, nineteenth-century portraits hanging from the walls, some small sculptures on the fireplace mantel, doors leading off into dark rooms at all four corners, and a wide, red-carpeted stairway upon which Aline, two tequilas ahead of anyone else, stretches out in her Japanese chintz dress.

Ysabel goes through the door behind the staircase and lights up the gallery retro-spective of abstract expressionist Juan Manuel de la Rosa. Separately now, paced according to caprice and inclination, each drifts through a series of connected rooms that culminate in a dark performance space. No one can find the light switch. Nevertheless, Ysabel is persuaded to sit at the piano while the others—American poet Mark Strand, Mexican poets Victor Manuel Mendiola, Aline Davidoff, and Jennifer Clement among them—sit scattered in the darkness. Ysabel plays several boleros and a ranchera by the beloved Mexican "musical poet" Agustín Lara. Jennifer and Victor get up

To dance across the stage, barely

visible, a satellite

trekking the night sky.

Gathered again in the foyer. Ysabel explains about the fossils in the glass cases. *Yes, they're from the abandoned mining town of Real de Catorce, where I've gone,* Ysabel says animatedly, *to participate in peyote ceremonies. I have a close friend there who collects ammonites and meteorite fragments.* No one should let the opportunity to visit Real de Catorce slip away, she insists, but Victor Manuel is rhapsodizing—through the garden en route back to the car—on the virtues of a nightcap, one more tequila.

Beside a sculpture, a wild-looking cactus with a spectacularly intricate flower—green sepals blown back from an explosion of white petals as delicate as a sea urchin and at its center, a feathery extrusion of thin yellow pistil and stamens. *A cereus,* Aline whispers as though she were afraid it might hear her. *Just once a year it blooms. In a few hours, at dawn, the flower will be wilted on that tendril like a tossed pair of panties.*

Just one tequila, Victor Manuel sings out. But it's two in the morning and the bars are closed. So Ysabel graciously extends an invitation to her house. No one protests, the Mexican night is endless. But no one is prepared for what is inside Ysabel's house.

It turns out, she has acquired one of the world's most extensive collections of anamorphoses, those distorted paintings that, viewed in a convex mirror or from a certain perspective, suddenly resolve into natural proportions. Flat on her living room table is a painting—like something made at the boardwalk by dripping liquid color onto a spinning square of cardboard. It is only when Ysabel places a cylindrical mirror at the center that a detailed image forms in the curve of the mirror: a fantastically gruesome scene of Christ on the cross. Next to the table, a contraption similar to a land surveyor's transit points toward a large painting of four faces. Ysabel notes that the man who commissioned the painting didn't want to be visible to his four enemies who are depicted in it. *Put your eye to the sight in the transit,* she directs, *and you will see the four faces resolve into one face, the face of the man who commissioned the work. His face is composed of the faces of his enemies who disappear that he might appear.*

Standing at the window across the room, Mark Strand points out a sheet of cloud illuminated from behind by the moon. While he watches, the cloud begins to disappear into some drawer of the night. The moon behind it follows, winking out, in a few seconds, altogether.

Lack of resolution suits Mexico. Objects, events, relationships, moments of self-consciousness, and—for the Maya—attendant spirits shift in and out of focus. Just as the anamorphic painting remains hidden until reflected on the surface of the convex mirror, Mexico withholds its plenum until unforeseeable circumstances reveal it.

Of course, every place is equally exotic and numbingly familiar, and our distance from others, as Edmond Jabès notes, is exactly that of our distance from ourselves. But for some cultures time is a mostly linear process. In Mexico, it is more circular. Mexico's most telling history and literature—Elena Poniatowska's *The Night of Tlatelolco,* Paco Ignacio Taibo's *'68,* and Juan Rulfo's *Pedro Páramo* being classic examples—are less characterized by cause and effect than by the various subjective experiences that make up living moments.

And Mexican time seems to have a different rhythm, flexibility, and capaciousness than *time* in the United States. Here, we continually feel time slipping away, we throw ourselves into work to get something done before time passes, the hours evaporate, we don't know where the day has gone. But in Mexico, some quality derived from the realities of Mexican life provides for an intuition of temporal layers, of one thing touching on another, of reflections and shifts in perspective, the interplay of presence and possibility, a dimension both quotidian and hallowed, the anguine twining of the visible and the invisible.

And maybe the relative ways that our cultures experience time has something to do with the ways we construe eros. In the United States, eros is so often presented as a noun: it is the image of an act into which the senses focus and exhaust themselves. But in Mexico, what is erotic is the transition, the ongoing slide from one strand of presence to another, approach and access, never the arrival. Mexican time is another form of *curiosity*—

An opening within an

opening, the event of a night-

blooming cereus.

THREE

EVAPORATION 3

How cold it looks on the yellow linoleum, she said.

Like watching a thumb war, he mumbled.

Spent the whole damn morning with the damn dishwasher man, she alerted him.

Standing in line watching the nape of the man in front of me, he remembered.

Perseid meteors from the radiant in the predawn, she read.

Is it really called Sutra of Angular Severity, he wondered.

Crossed out and then stetted, she noted.

High-speed dust fluorescing as it collides with solar wind, he read.

Now it's flu season, she wondered, should we give the boy an eye-wash?

They call it painting your throat, he explained, dipping the gauze in iodine.

In their component fatigue, the days… she mumbled.

And then you were talking in a French patois and wanting to go out, he said.

To be defiled is to be recognizable to yourself, she thought.

MOVING AROUND FOR THE LIGHT, A MADRIGAL

The natural order of things.

Sugar-bushing. Some

things we do would gross people out

because they just don't know. Always was

baffled by the connections in life. It's

moving around for the light. I thought,

that plant's growing before my eyes, it's insane.

What the news media don't want you

to know about. All the wild edible plants,

for instance. Getting on good here, blacks

and white. No fossil-fuel based technology. I've

eaten owl. Wing muscles and leg muscles,

that's the only meat on him.

So much roadkill—beavers,

otters, deer, raccoon.

We cook them up, preserve

the hide instead of slashing it. Got it

laid out real clear.

A lot can be done with duct tape. A bucket

of honey between May and August. Who

controls oil controls the world.

It's a lawyer's racket, but they don't go

by law. That's the truth and people don't even

know it. Want to find my bearings in

what's real. Started an anarchist collective with

    thirteen others. Like myself, independent people.

        Mountains seem to draw folks who want to live

in wilderness. The biggest problems come from being

    disconnected. I did really well in school, but

        I didn't like it. How do you sustain yourself day to day?

Take five milk goats and a sack of sweet potatoes.

    A grist mill, a harness shop. Most people

        independent enough to live out here like this,

they're too independent to listen to each other.

    Feed somebody lunch and they cut your wood

        all year—that works. Until

the kids are grown, don't want to

    bring others in. On account of influence.

        Some things we do would gross people out

because they don't know.

    Where do you think you come by your pattern

        for your ax handle? Take your old ax handle

and lay it on there. Nobody comes in,

    nobody leaves. We'll mind ourselves, let us alone.

        They wear people out so they say, I'll

just pay the fine. That's the truth

    and people don't even know it. I was on her windshield

        20 or 30 feet and then she hit the brakes

and I flew into a telephone pole.

    Heard a lot of stories about people's

        lives. Who needs a house and how much

tin? We're different, you can't treat us the same. Garlic,

    pumpkin, onions, squirrel. And they

        come to learn to make sorghum. Those that

have enough guts to live off the land, they are

    independent people like myself.

        But I lived in community. Lived with the Amish.

With them, wood-cutting isn't cutting wood,

    wood's a by-product. That's why you can't

        use chainsaws. Can't talk to someone

over a chainsaw. Want to move

    in a way that's more connected. See

        the cause and effect in my life.

Right at the start of my senior year. A natural

    progression from activism and travel. How do you

        sustain yourself day to day?

And people come to learn to make sorghum.

    What the news media don't want you

        to know. Those dogs, they're rabbit dogs. Like

to lose that feeling of being a foreigner and find

    a sense of being at home. Out

        felling trees alone on a windy day. Took my eyes

off it for 3 seconds, a big gust of wind came up

    and blew it down on me. My first thought

        was Oh shit I don't have insurance,

which is a really funny thought, considering.

    Let's get this process right.

        I'm not quitting unless I feel

in my heart I'm going to quit.

    That's the difference between me and other people.

        Blue heron is good, tastes good.

Ever eat a blue heron?

    Supervisor said there's no common law

        in Virginia. We don't know how fast it's going

to happen. Food's going to be

    number one. Next is going to be

        ammo. We figure we'll end up feeding

a lot of outsiders. Took my eye off it for 3 seconds.

    First thought was Oh shit. It's

        a right, it's always been a right.

The difference between me and other people.

    We'll care for ourselves, let us alone.

        I've got it laid out real clear.

Biggest problems come from being

    disconnected. Beavers, otters, deer, raccoon. I've

        eaten owl. Hard to feed yourself for a year.

Milk goats are the most valuable thing

        you can have. Banks go down, people can't get

            money, they'll see what they need.

Food's number one. And next

        is going to be ammo. If bad goes to worse,

            we'll post a man to keep out strangers.

Working to get that other doctor to move here. Like

        in Vietnam killing those women and kids, that's

            not the American mindset but

I think it might come to such. Tanning

        hides. Fire without matches. When

            others won't, we'll make it. Take

five milk goats and a sack of sweet

        potatoes, you can go anywhere. The

            natural order of things is when

a species gets dominant over its niche. I'm always

        baffled by the connections. That plant's

            growing before my eyes, it's —.

Instantly felt comfortable here.

        Skinned my first raccoon and it looked

            so much like a fetus I cried.

Don't know how fast it's going to happen or

        if it'll happen, but if it doesn't happen,

            we're not hurting either way.

Grew up using a bow and

      arrow to shoot rabbits. Need to be around

            like-minded people. So I can see

the cause and effect in my life.

      They're really strong personalities.

         I have a strong personality too.

Nobody comes in, nobody leaves. Ever

      eat a blue heron?

         Natural order of things.

Wing muscles and leg

      muscles. That's the only meat on him.

         Where do you think you come by your pattern?

Let's get this process right.

      Want to find my bearings in what's real.

         Move in a way that's more connected.

BOSNIA-HERZEGOVINA

LIFE IS WAITING

The magpie nearly invisible in the cherry tree eyes us we ascend the mountain's snaky dirt path toward the recently discovered Ice Age pyramid, the first pyramid ever found in Europe. That's the claim. The mountain is certainly shaped like a pyramid and we're told that sonar probes or infrared satellite images show clear structural evidence beneath hardpacked earth. There's not much activity on the mountain this afternoon, no tourists, no archeologists. And there is no way of telling which is the goat path and which is the path leading to the dig. Roma in the houses below are washing clothes on a terrace. Birdsongs intercept each other. Two small boys—no older than six or seven—appear and offer to lead us to the excavation site—across hillside and forest on no path whatsoever. When we get there, to a shallow muddy scrape, the boys disappear as suddenly—

It was a steep climb and we're sweating, out of breath and disappointed. The smokers among us light up. From the base of the first excavation, which exposes massive conglomerate slabs that look a lot to me, no expert on Bosnian pyramids, like natural metamorphic formations, we can gaze back down into Visočica, the city in the valley, clay tile and limestone slab roofs, six slender mosque towers, and a tight cluster of central buildings. Beyond, small houses embedded around the wooly neck of the next mountain and a scattering of structures against the green landscape below them. "Postmodernism," sighs Mladen, blowing the first breath of smoke out into the sultry afternoon air:

> "Five writers from three
>
> countries sit together
>
> with their backs to the pyramid."

A poet, he teaches library science in Sarajevo. From a mixed ethnic background, he was conscripted into the Bosnian military at the age of seventeen. Less than a year ago, he married a Muslim woman. Mario's demeanor is reflective, bordering on broody. The younger scholars describe him, half teasingly, half jealously, as someone who never stops studying. He identifies himself as a Bosnian and is quick to correct anyone who uses the general word Serb to reference the Serbian fascists, the Chetniks. He reminds me that some Serbs chose to remain in Sarajevo through the long years of shelling, the longest siege in modern history, and many died there. Even so, on the night we travel to Mostar where a restaurant's cynosural TV plays the European version of *American Idol*, he goes quiet when Serbia takes the lead and wins. Hearing people celebrating in the street, he mutters something bitter about the partying and the Serbs who killed seven thousand Bosnians at Srebrenica in a single day. The next evening, Mario's wife says to me, "It's curious that in his poems, he doesn't really address the war."

Towards the end of my time in Sarajevo, Mario and I are sitting at a table in the Writers' Center where a dedicated gnat is harassing us, buzzing around our eyes, angling off, veering back. "Did you know Bosnia is the only country without a McDonalds," he asks, smiling.

The gnat stalls

on his sleeve, vulnerable

at last to a swat.

But Mario gently, gently pushes the gnat off his sleeve with the tip of his finger. And as if to acknowledge this kindness, the gnat decamps, leaving us in peace.

With Mladen, a young translator, writer, and metal music enthusiast, I'm eating beef sausages called *ćevapčići* with onions and potatoes and an unreal ultra-cream, *kajmak,* at a café in the old part of town. During the war, Mladen's grandmother helped protect him with her stronghold of proverbs. When I ask him if he did, indeed, finish the mammoth novel he described to me the day before, he answers "No hair on my tongue." "What?" "A Bosnian expression—I'm telling the truth," he says. Mladen's novel is a riff on Norse mythology. As far as he knows, he says, he's one of the few young Bosnian writers fascinated by mythology; it is cognate with his love of science fiction. Jorge Luis Borges comes up in our conversation and Mladen magically pulls out a worn copy of Borges' stories from his back pocket. "As far as mythology goes," he says, "Bosnians generally distrust it on account of the way it was used by the Serbs during the war."

> Each conversation starts
>
> before, its taproot
>
> screwed into the war.

And yet, say the young Bosnians, they are sick of it—sick of all the art, films, literature, the whole of their lives ruddled with war.

"Don't you think it's necessary, the preoccupation with what happened?" I ask Mladen. He answers with another Bosnian proverb: "Yes, on the one hand, but on the other hand…"

Stubbing one cigarette out, Mladen lights up another. Smoking is the Bosnian national sport. Everywhere the poets meet to read or discuss poetics, we look across the room at each other through soiled gauze. "Look," he says, "this evening, you're going to try three clear alcohols: *rakija,* made from plum; *loza,* made from grapes; and *sljivovica,* from pear. The word for toast is *zivjeli.* You'll need to remember that much."

The Greek etymology of the word *enthusiasm* means "possessed by a god." The Bosnians use a similar word, *oduševljenje,* for those moments when, as poet Dijala Hasanbegovic says, "energies converge and you become all soul."

Mladen and Dijala walk us, the two American poets, to a little bookstore-café called Buy Book, still open although it is late and otherwise empty. We order Bosnian wine, *Carska Blatina*. Blatina from blato, mud, since the vineyards, we are told, thrive in a swampy plain. Mladen puts his smokes—Walter Wolf—on the table and the other American poet eyes them lustfully. "It's a Bosnian expression," Mladen offers: "What's on the table is for the table." He flicks his lighter.

The cigarette brands are one of the few things that seem to cut across nationalist lines. Bosnians smoke cigarettes made in Serbia, Croatia, and Bosnia. I see Walter Wolf, AurA, Moloko, Ronhill…, but just once Drina, the only brand of cigarettes available in Sarajevo during the siege when materials were so scarce that, according to Semezdin Mehmedinovic,

Drina cigarettes were sold

wrapped in pages torn from poetry books

(and, at least once, in a death certificate).

We wander out into the still city night and, close to the river, stumble onto the burned-out, lion-colored hulk of the National Library. After all these years, it is yet to be restored. At the front doors, a plaque memorializes the library's destruction by "Serbian criminals." On the side of the library, vivid in the moonlight, graffiti announces *Braco Voli Bedra*, Braco Loves Thighs. The two modes of registration, plaque and graffiti, historical wound and personal desire, clash in the soul of the Bosnians, sparking their famously morbid wit. Perhaps the most understated example of it will come in Mostar where, on a high, narrow bridge over white-crested rapids, someone has spray-painted the words *Zivot Je Cekanje*, Life Is Waiting. It isn't clear whether the passerby is being invited to reflect on the chasm or to leap into it.

There were those who grew rich and powerful on the war, as always. When the conflict ended, they were in position to control the political machinery. *Nekom rat, mekom brat,* the Bosnians say. Literally, *somebody war, somebody brother.* For those who suffered, war was like war; for those who thrived, war was like a brother.

These days, the religious and ethnic divisions are legislated into a transparently uneasy Serb and Croat/Muslim governing coalition. Tito's communism has been replaced by rampant nepotism. The remnants of an arcane bureaucracy, discouraging any permutation, much less innovation, swills the dreams of a younger generation which is marginalized, powerless, and underemployed. Socialism's "Everything belongs to me" attitude, the poet Pedja Kojovic suggests one late night at a cafe, reinforces wholesale corruption.

Many younger Bosnians have picked up English by watching TV. Those who grew up addicted to Latin American soap operas like *Esmerelda, Marisol,* and the long-running *La Usurpadora* starring Gabriela Spanic, a Mexican-Croatian actress, can often carry on in platitudinous Spanish.

In the Bosnian language, as in Japanese, every letter is pronounced.

Critical words,

heart and *death,*

take no vowels at all.

For the foreigner, a single word can become emblematic of the character of a country. In Portugal, it's *saudade,* a specifically Portuguese melancholy. In Spain, *duende. Kokoro* in Japanese combines qualities of heart and mind. In Bosnia, the signal word would be *sabur.* Translated as bearing, it more particularly characterizes the Bosnian attunement to the subtleties of life's rhythms.

Mujo: the character who is the butt of all jokes. Mujo goes into a bar and asks…

Beside the most significant Islamic building in the country, the Gazi Husrev-beg Mosque, originally built by an Ottoman architect in 1531, I stand under a massive horse chestnut and bend to drink from a fountain spilling water from the mosque's outer wall. Across the alley is the city's first public toilet, dating back to the Ottoman Empire. After taking a drink, I am told that, in accordance with local tradition, I must take on a Bosnian name. The one chosen for me by my band of Bosnian pranksters is Semsudin Gusic. Clearly, it is even more hilarious to them than my American name, although it means roughly the same thing, some equivalent of trees and duck.

> In the distance, on the huge bald
>
> hill overlooking Mostar, a deployment of white
>
> stones spells *Tito/ I love you.*

We go by bus from Mostar to Medjugorje where the Virgin Mary appeared, prompting the construction of a church and a much-needed tourist industry.

From Medjurgorje we ride to Počitelj, a fifteenth-century ruined castle built directly into a cliff face. Restored now as an artist's colony.

Rocky scrub yields to fertile valleys. Cherries are fruiting and poppies spackle the fields.

From Počitelj to Blagaj to visit a Dervish monastery built in the 1500s at the source—gushing from a cave at the bottom of an impressively vertical cliff—of the river Buna, one of the largest water sources in Europe. Above the monastery with its spare, carpeted prayer rooms, swallows inscribe their geometries in front of black-mouthed caves pocking the upper rock wall.

In Banja Luka, as the van circles downtown, filmmaker Senadin Musabegovic points out places where mosques once stood. Twenty mosques demolished without even a plaque to mark that they existed at all.

Mladen comments that Banja Luka is famous for its beautiful women. And for the architecture of its striking, orange-striped orthodox churches. In the evening, Senadin Musabegovic reads poems about his war experience in the poorly armed Bosnian army, about friends killed in the shelling. When he steps away from the mike, the scattered, polite applause from local Serbian-language poets registers only the withdrawal of a figure from a stage. Enthusiasm, no. No *oduševljenje.*

After we have eaten, the giant poet Admiral Mahic lurches through the dinner-time crowd toward me, his arms thrown out, his eyes wet, his voice booming affectionately: *Forrest Gander! I HATE you!*

Before lunch, Admiral Mahic, who gave an impassioned reading of a poem about a train and its travelers the evening before, stands up like a hill and grips my face between his meaty hands, his eyes moist, his voice roaring affectionately, *Forrest Gander! I HATE you!*

As I am heading down the stairs to the street, after working on translations of a poem by the young phenomenon Dijala Haganbesovic, Admiral Mahic spots me from across the room, raising his fist, his eyes gleaming, his bass voice filling the room with radiant affection: *Forrest Gander! I HATE you!*

FOUR

MAP OF THE WORLD

for Xi Chuan

Hank of yak hair plaited to the rearview mirror
And spicebush swallowtails feeding on raccoon scat.

I have to live with myself, she said, meaning nothing, really,
And what drew him to Goya's paintings were the open mouths.

Buzzards so engorged they have to vomit before they fly
And marbles in the concrete headstone spell *Child.*

Floodlights permanently blinding fish in the darkness
And he surgically removed the lips to beautify her pudenda.

They stood close enough to smell oils in the painting
As a million cicadas sucked roots beneath them.

Children ran from the collapsed houses, screaming
And a rain of cosmic dust thickens the pilot's cataracts.

It steps out of the night with razors in both hands
And the air conditioner blows warm germs over the bed.

Dolphins shrieking as they pierce the sardine shoal
And withdraw from description's false intimacy into what?

Hospitality's other face, hostility
And then stepped back, measuring him for a haymaker.

In the rubble of the siheyuan, washing his feet
While brake-residue smirches the bridge girders.

Each a stranger to the other's strangeness
And she strokes her horned toad in the direction of its spines.

Exact as the butcher's brass weights
And the water swells before it boils.

LOVEGREEN

That the trunk, submerged in air,

whirling leaves, thresholds-out. On the bark of

its leader stem, a black-capped

chickadee pins caterpillars and lacewings.

Its water-sprouts and spurs unpruned,

unbraced, the Yellow Transparent tree's

boughs release the girl open-mouthed

pumping her two-wheeler

across a meadow softly-furred

as a bumble bee, her plastic bag

pendant with hard apples

from one handlebar swaying—

Coffee cut with honeysuckle.

The unprimed pump won't give up its water.

Mosquito hawk clings to the barn wall's shadow.

✳   ✳   ✳

That the run-away breakdown of air, snagging itself

in the odor of mock orange. Or the girl in her daisy

dress, head held high and stiff as

an Awa doll

as she balances on a cable spool,

swollen with breath:

small triumph

summoned from the ongoing

blinking-out

of moments faithful to the sumac.

A song sparrow stops

anting its wing to fulfill

what silence wants, and look: the child's face,

her wet lips, her even teeth—

And the half-moon bone in her wrist.

A fairy door in the trunk of the oak.

Tadpoles beating upward to skim algae.

*   *   *

That as though pulling thread from a seam, the moment

reveals a child's elative glance

toward warbler-quickened birches

on an otherwise still morning

when all agrees to go quiet

but for the sound of leaves falling

through leaves,

the rotten, oily smell of red-blossoming

pawpaws clumped along the creek

where a boy muddies for fish with a gig and hoe.

The path diverges. To the left

and between tire ruts,

long mounds of spongy grass

swerve through trees, but to the right

the path not taken remains unknowable,

cottoned with light —

Soft-silted mouth of arrival.

A nest of shredded bark and small roots.

Croaking of the rain crow.

✶   ✶   ✶

That she, as though approaching

a speaking bush, tentative,

    crouches forward, and the toward-blowing tree

        vibrates-out

   through its tent of contour so

      no outline constrains it,

the slurry shadow

  pools across chromatic nuances of grass

      in wind—and

    she, supplicant as bent

  starlight, in midday's

slackening of birdsong, freezes.

    Our attention on the blithe

back of her. The moment

    rolls over like a log with a canthook

to reveal in the glow,

softly nudging her on,

    a place lying in wait for itself—

Fracture-porous base rock.

Chlorophyllous air sopping their laughter in.

They are hurling apples.

*　　*　　*

That squint-eyed of mind, the dog looks

where it will,

but the child, knock-kneed,

her arm planted like a cup handle,

faces the camera while

behind dog and girl, distance dissolves.

Darkness in the trees congeals.

Sound of summer running, an inconjugatable

verb, a memory supersaturated from which

this and this

drops out—

Chiastolite pebbles along the braided stream.

Smell of pine and camphor.

Clangor of light.

*   *   *

That she pours water from a pitcher

over her mother's hair, the leaves

flaring-up, the dog's

face blazed, in early emperor dusk.

The fragility of—, bird

perched at a branch's tip—

And later held her head in her hands

as though it could not contain itself.

The knapweed mowed, the Doric columns

remain hostage to vastation

and a sprig of ragwort in the foreground

utterly overcomes them.

Here as the idiom of *now* and *here* as

the incapacity

to call to mind

any music

whereof her face is not

inconceivably not the last note.

As if she had come to a corner of herself and were loitering.

Ecdysis, the shedding of an outer layer of skin.

From a doorway, looking out, a black Ancona rooster.

The crippled dog leans against the fence to bark.

CHILE

PIGS OF GOLD

Misreading the invitation. Not *Join us in Andacollo for the Festival of Cerdos de Oro,* pigs of gold, but for the *Festival of Cerros de Oro,* hills of gold. This year's topic: Poetry and Regionality.

Accepting the invitation, the U.S. poet arranges an all-day flight to Santiago and then a low-altitude sortie up the coast to La Serena, a neo-colonial town of churches and convents founded by Indian-killer Francisco de Aguirre in 1549 (ten years before the other, more notorious Aguirre launched his doomed expedition for El Dorado). From the scrappy municipal airport, a *regular taxi* curries the arrivant through streets flanked with white houses to the corner of Calle Domeiko and Avenida Francisco where he is deposited on the curb across from a muffler repair shop, there to wait until a *collective taxi* driver rustles up three more passengers bound for Andacollo. Unthinkable to drive with an empty seat. The foreign, a crossing place of languages and codes.

It's a squeeze and an hours-long ride through cactus plains and semi-desert mountain roads yielding glimpses of the snow-capped Andes, a languorous sine curve of a journey that ends with the brake-smoking descent into an abyss where the beleaguered town of Andacollo has been flung.

The universal getting-off place, La Iglesia de La Virgen del Rosario de Andacollo, is perimeterized by four adobe walls studded with ex-votos. Cut from marble and iron and sandstone, many are shaped like hearts, shields, and open books.

Thanks to the Virgin "por haber escuchado mis oraciones"—for having heard my prayers, "por salvar nuestro hijo"—for saving our child, "por el milagro concedido"—for the granted miracle. In an unusually specific ex-voto, a mother thanks the Virgin for helping her daughter turn from the demon of drugs. In another, the only one in English, Miriam offers

Thanks

For Forgive

My Fault.

The river is dry, a depository of bulging green plastic bags and noisome litter.

Andacollo: haunted by the ghosts of miners and gritty with tailings that blow from buzz-cut and beveled mountains, one behind the other into the horizon. An apocalyptic pastoral with micro-avalanches of sand serpentining in slow motion down sun-baked hills.

In cratered flats, tarry,

orange-fringed chemical

pools glisten.

In the miniature room where he is given lodge, the American poet sleeps with his suitcase on the bed; two feet away, his roommate snores like Beowulf.

Awake at 4 a.m., he steps into the street to check the stars and watches an old man bicycle past. Their glances catch and hold. Appraisal and plaidoyer and a judgement forever unknown. The bicycle quivers into a darkness that pours something alien into the core of the figure at the door. In the quick friction of mutual acknowledgment, a word is partially birthed. Curse or invitation? Who has penetrated deepest into the other's night? Why will one remember this moment so long?

Listen. The three thousand dog nights of Andacollo.

At dinner, the Santiago poet averts her face from the gringo although no one else is sitting close enough for her to engage in conversation. A synecdoche, he is taken for his government. She lights up and blows sullen smoke down the table. With suspicion at the threshold of dialogue, there is always a word blocking the first word.

And on the second day of the festival, after many papers, a consensus emerges that there are no longer *regions* of poetry; there are *zones*. A distinction weakened, perhaps, in translation?

Final night, a local poet accuses the host of avoiding the issue of regionality altogether, of talking around it with clever language games when, in fact, some people's lives are at risk, even now, at this moment, because of what they write, because of where they live.

Another shouts from the audience that vanguard poetry doesn't speak to him, it is elitist, the tone of the whole conference is elitist.

And so the last evening dissolves into tensions,

A dinner table balanced

like a barbell, partisan drinkers

clustered at either end.

The foreigner can't control his situation; mastery eludes him. After four days in another language, he who started out *infinitely sensitive* is *completemente rendido*, rent by the effort of constant attentiveness.

The gift of books cannot be refused, despite there is zero room in his suitcase. *Arigato-meiwaku*, Bashō would say as he hiked through villages accumulating gifts he could not humanly carry. *Thanks, but no thanks.*

Walking beside his young wife, the *paisano* steers, with a menacing glare, the eyes of the foreigner away from her.

Before reaching the Virgin's sanctum in the church, pilgrims pass displays of gifts from abroad. Samurai armor. Hammered silver spoons. A red robe from Kenya. Chinese banners. All sent in praise of the Virgin of Andacollo.

The last daylight spiders down from a small ring of stained glass in the ceiling. According to legend, a peasant found this figure of the Virgin, carved and pristine, lying—waiting—in the wilderness.

She stands three feet high on a small platform looking down into the nave of the church, the empty pews. There is a pull rope connecting the Virgin of Andacollo to the grate that protects her from visitors to her sanctum. One must kneel to pull the rope and see the Virgin

> Slowly, without
>
> creaking, swivel to
>
> face the visitor.

She too awakens the unknown inside him. A white, silken, isosceles gown, strung with loops of amethyst, covers her from neck to feet. Her wooden head is topped with a golden crown. From her slightly out-turned ears, two leaf-shaped earrings dangle. One of her brown eyes looks sleepily ahead while the other focuses down.

When fog covers Andacollo, says the barkeep, someone is about to die.

> Cigarette butts
>
> surround the bare twig in the
>
> sand of the flowerpot.

And those things that look like stupas on the hills around Andacollo? A cult of Tibetan monks, says the barkeep, but the unlikely story evaporates into the night.

For a while, linguistic fluency may be bluffed with a good accent and fast delivery, but speed leads to grammatical mistakes and embarrassment from which the speaker can only emerge, like a gambler playing the Martingale, by doubling the speed and then the mistakes until he finds himself fallen into a well below the world of human voices. So the one who was hosted becomes hostage.

One night, he rides a bus to La Silla, The Saddle, an observatory bordering the southern extremity of the Atacama Desert. Trundles into the high, cold, desert night with others to look through a telescope at a constellation named for a parrot. *Cuernos de cabra* in bloom all around,

The night fragrant, windless,

holding afloat a low

mmm of conversations.

When the mines played out and companies folded, a few families remained and dug for whatever might have been left behind. Then they too disbanded. The town began to crumble. This four-man wildcat operation has likewise begun to fail or never stopped failing and so the owner, his gums mottled and brown, flecks of saliva at the corner of his mouth—a sign of mercury poisoning—welcomes rare tourists. In the sear of afternoon sun, one miner is crushing stone, another scooping the pieces into a rudimentary wooden sieve. The owner steps under a tin roof where sieved gravel is swirled in large washtubs. From his pocket, he takes a vial and pours several beads of quicksilver, mercury, across the life-line of his palm. He smears this against a tin plate he attaches to the washtub. After swishing the muddy water with a paddle, he removes the metal plate, flecked now with gold precipitate. This he wipes into a cloth filter, again with his bare hand.

A door is a door. So says poet Raúl Zurita in dispraise of abstraction. And maybe torture (*now that everything in your life has changed*) inclines survivors, like Zurita, toward identification with the tangible world.

He says in those days of brutality, distrust, and terror, the reign of Pinochet, he began to imagine writing poems in the sky, on the faces of cliffs, in the desert. A city poet all of his life, he began to dream of nature. He started to imagine fighting sadistic force with poems as insubstantial as contrails over a city.

His words *Ni Pena, Ni Miedo* (Neither Shame Nor Fear), bulldozed into the sand of the Atacama Desert, would gradually fade away joining thousands of men, women, and children who disappeared in shame and fear during the Pinochet years. But schoolchildren from the closest pueblo come with shovels and turn over the ground inside the letters, refreshing them. And so, in situ, new editions of the poem are published.

Zurita's remarkable presence. His nose, expressive as a collie's, marks him for melancholy. His grandmother was Italian and he talks with his hands. His face, tense with gravitas, suddenly zooms forward, breaking into a smile, a laugh that issues from the whole of him. The warmth he emits. But even after his recent operation, *it was nothing,* he still has four kidney stones and doesn't look comfortable on the hard wooden seat at the small breakfast table in The Orly Hotel.

In the Plaza de Armas,

> A cannon sends shock waves through my shirt,
> the pigeons whoosh into the air,
> a spadeful of exploding fists.

A little girl with a balloon giraffe grips her mother's hand.

The bus lets him off. Classic comic scene: the travel-bedraggled foreigner on a dusty road looking in either direction for a sign. Then he is dragging his luggage through tawny dirt toward Restaurant Veinte Poemas de Amor. How, now he's come all this way without an address, is he going to find Nicanor Parra, the nonagenarian Chilean anti-poet? He orders lunch and glances idly at folk art on the wall. One painting, decorated with shells, represents a simplified map of Isla Negra. Below a square house on the main road, the artist has written *Neruda*. At the end of the road that curves along the boundary river, another house is labeled *Parra*.

> *Donde una puerta*
>
> *se cierra, otra*
>
> *se abre.*

He is the only guest at a hostel called La Casa Azul. The caretaker, an Argentine painter, shows him through the kitchen—coffee and oranges—and to his room. Yes, yes, the Argentine knows the famous poet Nicanor Parra. In fact, Parra's writing studio is just up the road. But Parra doesn't actually live in Isla Negra. He lives two towns distant.

Flagging, the wayfarer trudges back to the main street to bargain with a taxi driver. Yes, yes, the driver knows the famous poet Parra and the town where he lives. Twenty minutes away. But when they arrive at Las Cruces, the driver slows to ask the first person he sees where Nicanor Parra lives.

A gated house, butted against the sea. He leaps out with books, gifts, a note, in case Parra isn't there, explaining that he is an admirer come this long way in hope of meeting even briefly, suggesting that if Don Parra wants to fall together, he might leave a message at La Casa Azul in Isla Negra. The *muchacha* sticks her head out from behind the door and tells him No, he cannot see Parra. Is she sure? She is sure. He asks if he can leave the gifts and the note. She takes them and closes the door in the same fluid gesture, and he goes back to the running taxi and waits, hoping that Parra might read the note and step out to greet him. No luck. The taxi driver, commiserating, takes him back to Isla Negra. At La Casa Azul, he alerts the painter that he is expecting a call from Nicanor Parra. A call, the painter says, perplexed. We have no phone here.

Abandoning all hope, as has been written, he decides to look at Neruda's house before it closes, and he walks over and pays for the tour. Rooms of ship figureheads, collections of shells, a narwhal tusk, African masks, hand-carved furniture, broad rafters carved with names of his dead friends. All museum quality. Back at La Casa Azul, darkness contracts. The painter sees him making for his room. Oh, the painter says in Spanish, Don Parra came to see you. Drove here by himself in his orange VW and came to the door with some books.

Did he leave the books, a message, anything?

He just said, Tell them that I came.

There is a poem by Walter de la Mare about a man who gallops his horse to a ramshackle mansion on a dark night and, when no one responds to his pounding, shouts up at the windows, *Tell them that I came.* Parra, who knows English poetry well, might have been quoting that poem. There are Chinese poems, too, written by disciples who hiked into mountains to visit a master and waited and finally left without making contact. None of the literary precedents, which the traveler recalls from his bunk in the cold, dark room, comforts him.

He takes himself to the good restaurant, a mindful guest. But

> The bowl of local
>
> shellfish called *locos*
>
> tastes like steamed thumbs.

The waiter's strange, serious manner might be mistaken for contempt, but it gradually comes clear that he's trying to make an impression with the rigor of his hospitality.

Next morning, there is the sleathy stranger, standing on the street waiting for a bus to Valparaiso. Sidling toward him, a pitiful, matted dog with a hairless tail. It rolls onto its back offering its belly, revealing a black testicular tumor the size of a tennis ball. Chewed open to the raw pink tissue deep within.

Across from the bar, he is seated in a alcove in the wall just capacious enough for the tiny table and two chairs. Neruda was a denizen here, he is informed, as he is so informed in every Chilean bar. The waiter warns him not to hit his head when he stands, which, on two occasions an hour apart, he nevertheless manages to do.

Valparaiso. Pastel city of hills with narrow, spooling cobblestone streets. Jungled gullies hemmed by technicolor houses of tin, wood, native stone. Burned ruins and dreamy casitas with views of the bay, side by side.

Viña Tarapacá, the waiter announces proudly, Ex Zavala, 2002, Cabernet. Third best wine in Chile. The guitar player in the corner strums a song written by Violeta Parra, the celebrated poet's sister: *Gracias a la vida que me ha dado tanto.* Who can listen to Parra's song without shedding their self-concern, their burden of gripes?

> Though the path to the bar reeks
>
> of cat urine, the men's room dispenser
>
> serves chocolate condoms.

At Neruda's Valparaiso house, cylinders of music are stacked on his writing desk. Polka, *The Barber of Seville, L'Angelus de la Mer,* and *Los Tribulaciones d'un Pipelet.*

An unconceived ingress, he stumbles upon a back-alley haunt in which the names of thousands of passers-through are scribbled with markers and pens across everything—the walls, cabinets of antiques, windows—and photos of these innumerable pilgrims are stuck into every picture frame and mirror, obscuring whatever else once appeared there. A dark shrine memorializing those who are not at home. He orders the country's third best wine.

A bent man in a baggy suit enters, leaves, returns, smiles, approaches a young couple eating, goes out again, returns and mimes clapping his hands. And then from a shelf of antiques in a corner of the restaurant, the old man plucks up two gourds. An accordianist emerges from the kitchen and sits on a chair by the door and begins to play, swaying, while his companion shakes the gourds and breaks into song—something to do with butterflies coming out of someone's mouth with end-words that rhyme, in Spanish, *Valparaiso* and *I adore you.* More people crowd in. The gringo orders another round.

At the next table, two young lovers, eating the traditional dish of steak over French fries, clap when the last song in the set ends. The packed room joins in the clapping.

Putting down the gourds, the singer drops a battered envelope on the table and winds his way around the tables, greeting those he knows with boisterous exclamations. The air is smoky, the voices loud, the envelope says, *Gracias por su valiosa cooperación.* The foreigner puts in a few bills and asks in a low shout for a tango—the musician cups his hand to his ear—he shouts again. The singer nods to the accordianist, three generations of a family file through the door and disperse into the chaos, the musicians launch into a song called *El Indio Vigoroso,* more town people arrive, bottles appear and disappear from the tables, the room is mobbed and raucous, the thousands of hand-scrawled names pulsing on the walls, the multitude of photographs staring fixedly at the living, he takes off his jacket, his eyes slanted, unblinking, reptilian. He stands, wobbling, to try to make his way toward the toilet, but the space in the room is contracting, expanding. And yet it seems to him that at last he's in rhythm with the local, at home, that the foreign has rendered itself accessible and his life is taking place in real time in the place where he has arrived. Immediately he finds himself alone in the alley kneeling on cobblestones while behind him, within the throbbing, roaring cantina,

The Valparaisan night

copies his face and signs

his name to the wall.

ACKNOWLEDGMENTS

*The author gratefully acknowledges the
magazines and chapbooks in which this
work first appeared:*

"Evaporation 1" appeared as "Ligature 5"
in *American Poet,* Spring 2007, edited by
Jennifer Kronovet.

"A Clearing" was published in *A Clearing,*
photographs by Raymond Meeks, Nazraeli
Press, 2008, and in *Almost Island,* 2008,
edited by Sharmistha Mohanty and
Vivek Narayanan.

An earlier version of "Xinjiang: The Pamirs
Poetry Journey" appeared in *American
Poetry Review,* August/September 2008,
edited by Elizabeth Scanlon.

"Evaporation 2" appeared in *Boston Review,*
May 2009, edited by Timothy Donnelly.

Parts of "The Tinajera Notebook" appeared
in *Conjunctions* 49, Fall 2007, edited by
Bradford Morrow.

An earlier version of "Mexico: A Core
Sample through 24 Hours" appeared in
American Poetry Review, March/April 2008,
edited by Elizabeth Scanlon.

"Evaporation 3" appeared as "Ligature 7"
in *Conjunctions* 48, Fall 2006, edited by
Bradford Morrow.

"Moving Around for the Light: A Madrigal" appeared in *Lyric,* Summer 2009, edited by Nathaniel Perry.

An earlier version of "Bosnia-Herzegovina: Life Is Waiting" appeared as "Report from Bosnia-Herzegovina" in *American Poetry Review,* September/October 2008, edited by Elizabeth Scanlon.

"Evaporation 4" was included as "Map of the World" in the exhibition "Earth Visions/ *Visiones Terrestres*" at Swem Library, The College of William & Mary, March 2008.

"Lovegreen" appeared in *Sound of Summer Running,* photographs by Raymond Meeks, Nazraeli Press, 2004; as "Of Sum" in *EcoPoetry,* Spring 2009, edited by Jonathan Skinner; and in *Angelaki,* Spring 2009, guest edited by Kate Fagan, John Kinsella, and Peter Minter.

An earlier version of "Chile: Pigs of Gold" appeared in *Conjunctions* 46, Spring 2006, edited by Bradford Morrow; the section concerned with Nicanor Parra appeared in *Brick,* April 2008, edited by Michael Redhill.

Thank you to the photographers:

SECTION ONE
Photographs by Raymond Meeks from *A Clearing* (Nazraeli Press, 2008). Used with permission.

SECTION TWO
Photographs by Graciela Iturbide. Used with permission.

SECTION THREE
Photographs by Lucas Foglia from his series "Rewilding." Used with permission.

SECTION FOUR
Photographs by Raymond Meeks from *Sound of Summer Running* (Nazraeli Press, 2004). Used with permission.

Thanks to Kent Johnson, my companion on the hejira to Andacollo and Sarejevo, and to Eliot Weinberger, my companion on the Pamirs journey. "The friends thou hast, and their adoption tride..."

Thanks also to the John Simon Guggenheim Memorial Foundation and to United States Artists for their significant support.